Simply Stars
Easy Quilts & Projects

by Landauer Publishing

Landauer Publishing, LLC

Simply Stars
Easy Quilts & Projects

This book was designed, produced,
and published by Landauer Publishing, LLC
3100 101st Street, Urbandale, IA 50322
www.landauerpub.com
515/287/2144 800/557/2144

President/Publisher: Jeramy Lanigan Landauer

Vice President of Sales and
Administration: Kitty Jacobson

Editor: Jeri Simon

Art Director: Laurel Albright

Photographer: Sue Voegtlin

ISBN 13: 978-1-935726-70-8

This book printed on acid-free paper.

Printed in United States

10-9-8-7-6-5-4-3-2-1

FACEBOOK.COM/LANDAUERPUBLISHING YOUTUBE.COM/LANDAUERPUBLISHING PINTEREST.COM/LANDAUERPUB

Table of Contents

Spotted Stars Wallhanging.............. 4

Lemon Stars Quilt............................ 8

Twilight Sky Quilt 12

The Color of Stars Wallhanging......16

Star Table Square...........................20

Star Studded Table Runner 24

Jane's Star Garden Quilt 28

Star Steps Quilt 34

Projects inspired by Lynette Jensen's timeless patterns and recreated with today's fabrics.

Wallhanging recreated by Jeri Simon; quilted by E.B. Updegraff

Inspired by Fancy Flywheels Wallhanging in Thimbleberries® Quilts for My Sister's House by Lynette Jensen.

Spotted Stars

Wallhanging

Finished size: 34" square

Materials

1/2 yard large floral print fabric for fussy cut block centers

1/4 yard white print fabric for blocks

1/4 yard orange multi-dot fabric for blocks

1/2 yard light blue fabric for blocks

1/3 yard white multi-dot fabric for blocks and lattice post squares

1/2 yard teal fabric for lattice segments

1/3 yard stripe fabric for binding

1-1/4 yards backing fabric

40" square batting

Fabric quantities based on 42"-44"-wide 100% cotton fabrics.

wof=width of fabric

Sew with a 1/4" seam allowance unless otherwise stated.

Cutting

From large floral print fabric,
fussy cut: (4) 3-1/2" squares

Note: I centered a flower in each square

From white print fabric, cut:
(3) 2" x wof strips. From the strips cut:
(8) 2" x 3-1/2" rectangles
(8) 2" x 6-1/2" rectangles

From orange multi-dot fabric, cut:
(1) 3-7/8" x wof strip

From light blue fabric, cut:
(1) 3-7/8" x wof strip
(2) 3-1/2" x wof strips. From the strips cut:
(16) 3-1/2" squares

From white multi-dot fabric, cut:
(3) 3-1/2" x wof strips. From 2 strips cut:
(16) 3-1/2" squares
From the remaining strip cut:
(9) 3-1/2" lattice post squares

From teal fabric, cut:
(4) 3-1/2" x wof strips. From the strips cut:
(12) 3-1/2" x 12-1/2" lattice segments

From stripe fabric, cut:
(4) 2-1/2" x wof strips for binding

Block Assembly

1. With right sides together, sew 2" x 3-1/2" white print rectangles to opposite sides of a 3-1/2" large floral print square. Press.

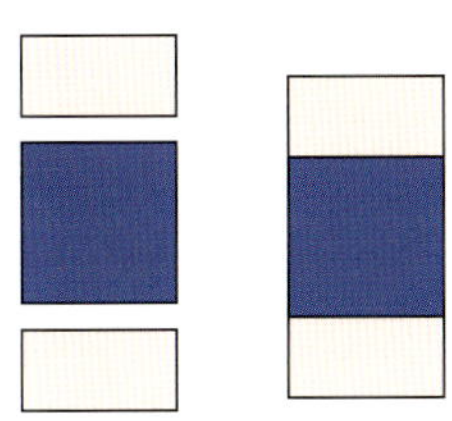

2. With right sides together, sew 2" x 6-1/2" white print rectangles to the remaining sides of the large floral print square in step 1. Press to make a 6-1/2" block center. Make 4 block centers.

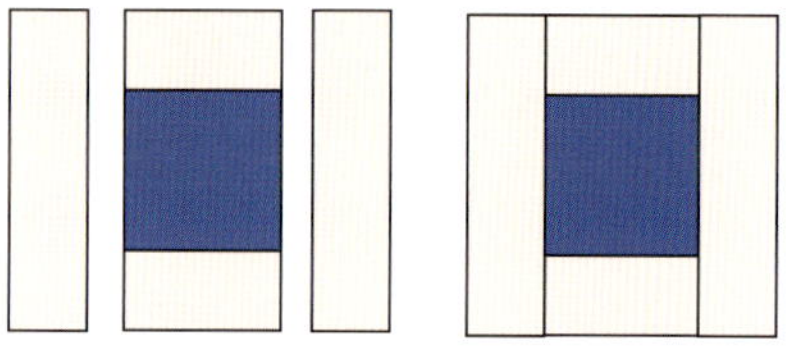

Make 4

3. With right sides together, layer the 3-7/8" x wof orange multi-dot print and light blue strips together. Press. Cut the layered strips into 3-7/8" squares. Cut the squares in half diagonally to make 16 sets of triangles.

Make 16

4. Stitch 1/4" from the long edge of each set of triangles. Press the triangles open to make (16) 3-1/2" half-square triangles.

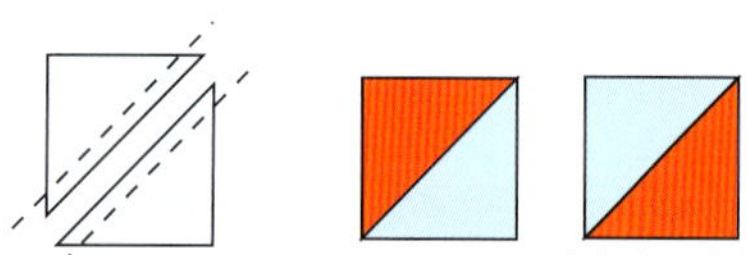

Make 16

5. Sew a 3-1/2" white multi-dot square to the left edge of each half-square triangle as shown. Press. Make 16 units.

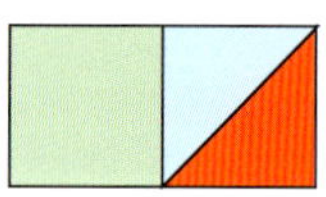

Make 16

6. Referring to the diagram, sew a unit to the top and bottom edges of each block center. Press.

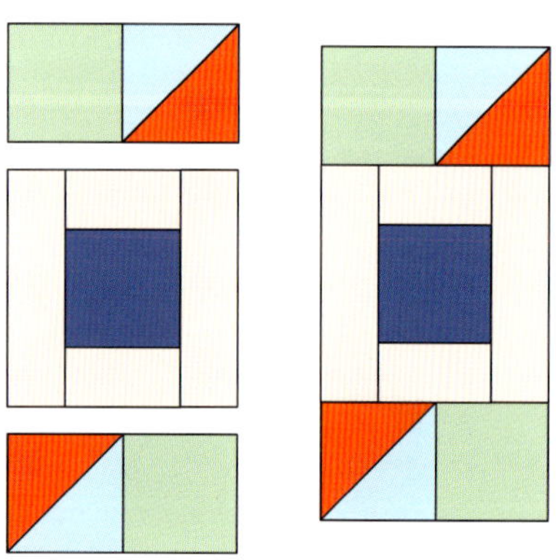

7. Sew 3-1/2" light blue squares to the ends of the remaining step 5 units. Press.

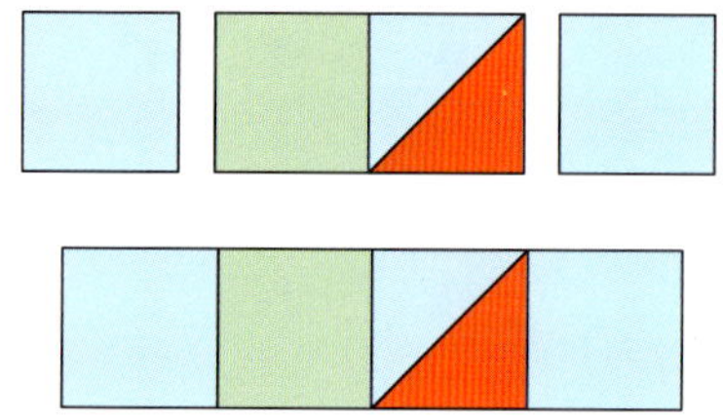

8. Sew the step 7 units to the remaining sides of the block center. Press to make a block. Make (4) 12-1/2" blocks.

Make 4

Wallhanging Assembly

1. Lay out (3) 3-1/2" x 12-1/2" teal lattice segments and 2 blocks in a row as shown. Sew the pieces together to make a block row. Press the seam allowances toward the lattice segments. Make 2 block rows.

Make 2

2. Lay out (2) 3-1/2" x 12-1/2" teal lattice segments and (3) 3-1/2" white multi-dot lattice post squares in a row as shown. Sew the pieces together to make a sashing row. Press the seam allowances toward the lattice segments. Make 3 sashing rows.

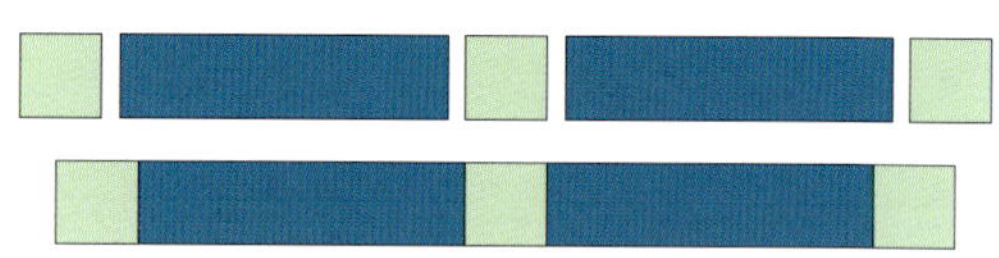

Make 3

3. Referring to the diagram, lay out the block and sashing rows as shown.

4. Sew the rows together, pinning at the seam intersections as needed. Press the seam allowances in one direction.

Finishing the Wallhanging

1. Layer the backing, batting and wallhanging top. Baste the layers together and hand or machine quilt.
2. Sew the binding strips together to make one continuous strip. Press the strip in half, wrong sides together, along the length. Sew the binding to the edges of the wallhanging. Turn the binding over the edge to the back of the wallhanging and hand or machine stitch in place.

Quilt recreated by McB McManus;
quilted by E.B. Updegraff

Inspired by Holiday Stars Quilt in Thimbleberries® New Collection of Classic Quilts by Lynette Jensen.

Lemon Stars

Quilt

Finished size: 65" square

Materials

1-1/4 yards light gray floral print fabric for blocks, lattice post squares and sawtooth border

1-3/4 yards light gray dot fabric for background, inner border and sawtooth border

1-1/3 yards dark gray print fabric for blocks, middle border and binding

1-5/8 yards yellow print fabric for blocks and outer border

2/3 yard white dot fabric for lattice segments

4 yards backing fabric

71" square batting

Fabric quantities based on 42"-44"-wide 100% cotton fabrics.

wof=width of fabric

Sew with a 1/4" seam allowance unless otherwise stated.

Cutting

From light gray floral print fabric, cut:
- (9) 2-1/2" x wof strips. From 5 strips cut:
  - (72) 2-1/2" block squares
  - From 1 strip cut:
  - (16) 2-1/2" lattice post squares
- (4) 2-7/8" x wof strips for sawtooth border

From light gray dot fabric, cut:
- (12) 2-1/2" x wof strips. From 8 strips cut:
  - (72) 2-1/2" x 4-1/2" rectangles
  - From 1 strip cut:
  - (4) 2-1/2" corner squares for sawtooth border
- (5) 2-1/2" x wof strips for inner border
- (4) 2-7/8" x wof strips for sawtooth border

From dark gray print fabric, cut:
- (4) 2-1/2" x wof strips. From the strips cut:
  - (36) 2-1/2" x 4-1/2" rectangles
  - (7) 2-1/2" x wof strips for binding
- (6) 1" x wof middle border strips

From yellow print fabric, cut:
- (1) 4-1/2" x wof strip. From the strip cut:
  - (9) 4-1/2" squares
- (7) 6-1/2" x wof outer border strips

From white dot fabric, cut:
- (8) 2-1/2" x wof strips. From the strips cut:
  - (24) 2-1/2" x 12-1/2" lattice segments

Star Block Assembly

1. Place a 2-1/2" light gray floral print square on one corner of a 2-1/2" x 4-1/2" light gray dot rectangle, right sides together. Draw a diagonal line, corner to corner, on the wrong side of the square. Stitch on the drawn line. Trim the seam allowance to 1/4" and press. Repeat with another 2-1/2" light gray floral print square on the opposite corner of the rectangle. Press to make a flying geese unit. Make 36 flying geese units.

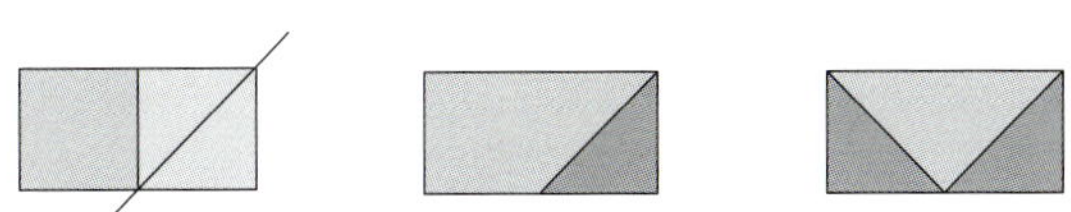

Make 36

2. Sew a 2-1/2" x 4-1/2" dark gray print rectangle to the bottom edge of each flying geese unit. Press. Make 36.

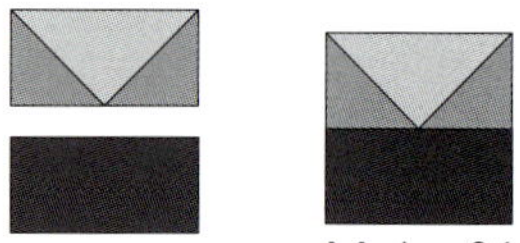

Make 36

3. Layer the light gray floral print and light gray dot 2-1/2" x wof strips right sides together. Sew the strips together along one long edge. Press open to make a strip set. Make 3 strip sets. Cut the strip sets into (36) 2-1/2"-wide segments.

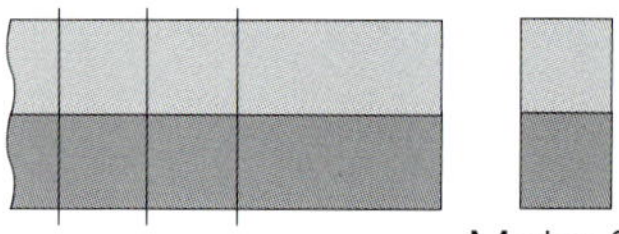

Make 36

4. Sew a 2-1/2" x 4-1/2" light gray dot rectangle to the bottom edge of each 2-1/2" segment. Press.

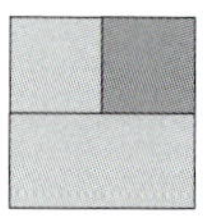

5. Sew units from step 2 to opposite sides of a 4-1/2" yellow print square. Press to make a 4-1/2" x 12-1/2" block center unit. Make 9 block center units.

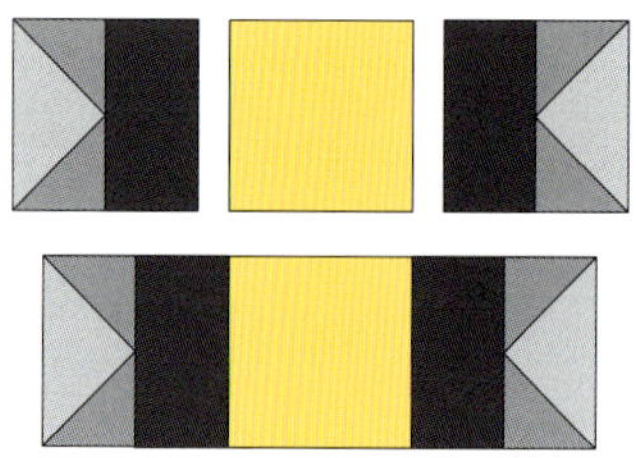

Make 9

6. Sew units from step 4 to the side edges of the remaining step 2 units. Press to make a 4-1/2" x 12-1/2" top/bottom block unit. Make 18 top/bottom block units.

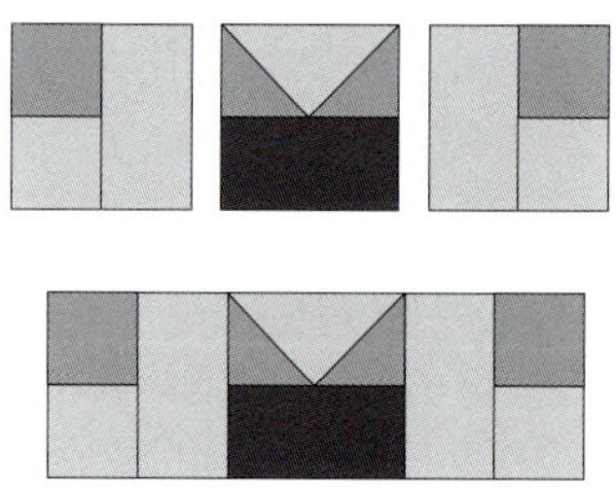

Make 18

7. Sew a top/bottom block unit to the top and bottom of the block center unit. Press to make a 12-1/2" star block. Make 9 star blocks.

Make 9

Quilt Center Assembly

1. Lay out (3) 2-1/2" x 12-1/2" white dot lattice segments and (4) 2-1/2" light gray floral print lattice post squares in a row as shown. Sew the pieces together to make a sashing row. Press the seam allowances toward the lattice segments. Make 4 sashing rows.

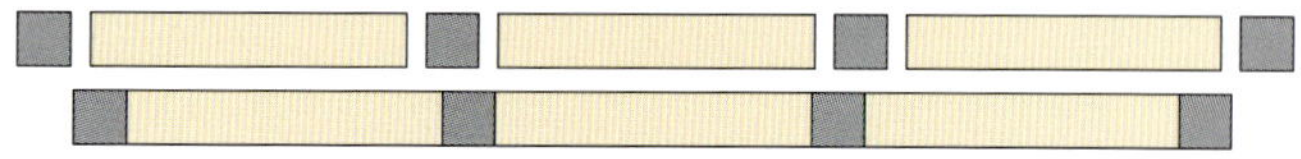

Make 4

2. Lay out 3 star blocks and (4) 2-1/2" x 12-1/2" white dot lattice segments in a row as shown. Sew the pieces together to make a block row. Press the seam allowances toward the lattice segments. Make 3 block rows.

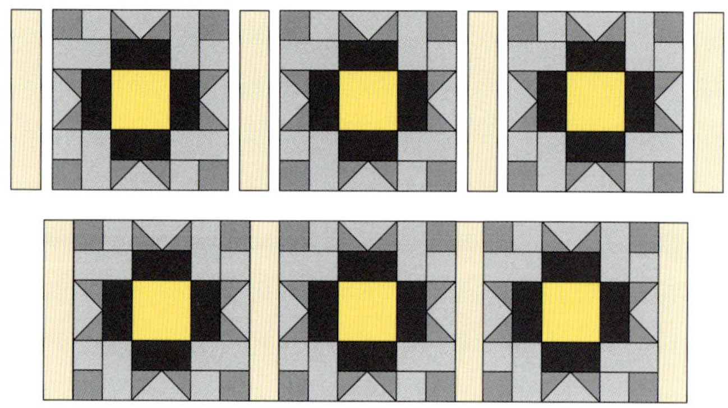

Make 3

3. Referring to the Quilt Diagram on page 11, lay out the block and sashing rows as shown. Sew the rows together, pinning at the seam intersections as needed. Press the seam allowances in one direction. The quilt center should measure 44-1/2" square.

Border Assembly

1. Sew the (5) 2-1/2" light gray dot inner border strips together to make one continuous strip. Measure the quilt center from side to side through the middle and cut a top and bottom border to this length. Sew the top and bottom borders to the quilt center. Press.

2. Measure the quilt center from top to bottom through the middle. Include the top and bottom borders in this measurement. Cut two side borders to this length. Sew the side borders to the quilt center. Press.

3. Layer the light gray dot and light gray floral print 2-7/8" x wof strips right sides together. Press. Cut the layered strips into (48) 2-7/8" squares. Cut the squares in half diagonally to make 96 sets of triangles.

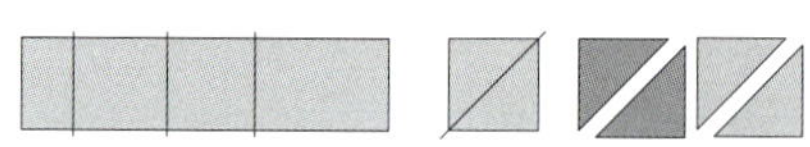

Make 96

4. Stitch 1/4" from the long edge of each set of triangles. Press the triangles open to make (96) 2-1/2" half-square triangles.

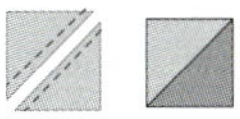

Make 96

5. Referring to the Quilt Diagram, sew 24 half-square triangles together to make a top/bottom sawtooth border. Make 2 top/bottom sawtooth borders. Sew the sawtooth border strips to the top/bottom edges of the quilt center. Press.

Note: Pay attention to how the half-square triangles change direction at the center of the border.

6. Referring to the Quilt Diagram, sew 24 half-square triangles together to make a side sawtooth border. Add a 2-1/2" light gray dot corner square to each end of the side sawtooth border. Press. Sew the sawtooth border strips to the side edges of the quilt center. Press.

Note: Pay attention to how the half-square triangles change direction at the center of the border.

7. Referring to steps 1-2, sew the 1" dark gray print middle border strips and the 6-1/2" yellow print outer border strips to the quilt center. Press.

Finishing the Quilt

1. Cut the backing fabric in half crosswise to make (2) 2 yard lengths. Using a 1/2" seam allowance, sew the pieces together along one long edge. Press seam open.
2. Layer the backing, batting and quilt top. Baste the layers together and hand or machine quilt.
3. Sew the binding strips together to make one continuous strip. Press the strip in half, wrong sides together, along the length. Sew the binding to the edges of the quilt. Turn the binding over the edge to the back of the quilt and hand or machine stitch in place.

Quilt Diagram

Quilt recreated and quilted by E.B. Updegraff;
pieced by McB McManus

Inspired by Midnight Sky Quilt in Thimbleberries® Collection of Classic Quilts by Lynette Jensen.

Twilight Sky

Quilt

Finished size: 48" x 60"

Materials

1 yard orange solid fabric for blocks

1 yard white solid fabric for blocks

1-1/2 yards light aqua solid fabric for blocks and binding

1 yard dark teal solid fabric for blocks

3-1/2 yards backing fabric

52" x 64" batting

Fabric quantities based on 42"-44"-wide 100% cotton fabrics.

wof=width of fabric

Sew with a 1/4" seam allowance unless otherwise stated.

Cutting

From orange solid fabric, cut:

- (14) 2-1/2" x wof strips. From 4 strips cut:
  - (36) 2-1/2" squares
  - (2) 2-1/2" x 6-1/2" rectangles
  - (16) 2-1/2" x 4-1/2" rectangles

From white solid fabric, cut:

- (13) 2-1/2" x wof strips. From 3 strips cut:
  - (24) 2-1/2" squares
  - (8) 2-1/2" x 6-1/2" rectangles
  - (4) 2-1/2" x 4-1/2" rectangles

From light aqua solid fabric, cut:

- (20) 2-1/2" x wof strips. From 4 strips cut:
  - (36) 2-1/2" squares
  - (2) 2-1/2" x 6-1/2" rectangles
  - (16) 2-1/2" x 4-1/2" rectangles

Note: 6 strips will be used for binding.

From dark teal solid fabric, cut:

- (13) 2-1/2" x wof strips. From 3 strips cut:
  - (24) 2-1/2" squares
  - (8) 2-1/2" x 6-1/2" rectangles
  - (4) 2-1/2" x 4-1/2" rectangles

Star Unit Assembly

1. Place a 2-1/2" orange solid square on each corner of a 2-1/2" x 6-1/2" white rectangle, right sides together. Draw a diagonal line, corner to corner, on the wrong side of the squares. Stitch on the drawn lines as shown. Trim the seam allowances to 1/4" and press. Refer to the diagram when stitching the squares. Press to make an orange/white/orange center unit. Make 8 orange/white/orange center units.

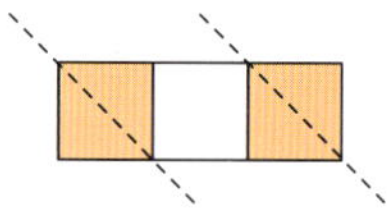

Make 8

2. Referring to step 1, make 2 white/orange/white center units, 8 light aqua/dark teal/light aqua center units and 2 dark teal/light aqua/dark teal center units.

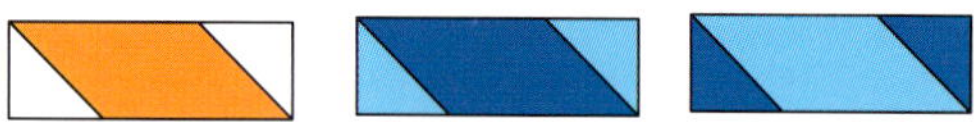

Make 2 Make 8 Make 2

3. Place a 2-1/2" white solid square on the corner of a 2-1/2" x 4-1/2" orange rectangle. Draw a diagonal line, corner to corner, on the wrong side of the square. Stitch on the drawn line as shown. Trim the seam allowance to 1/4" and press. Sew a 2-1/2" orange square to the white side of the unit, as shown. Press to make an orange/white outer unit. Make 16 orange/white outer units.

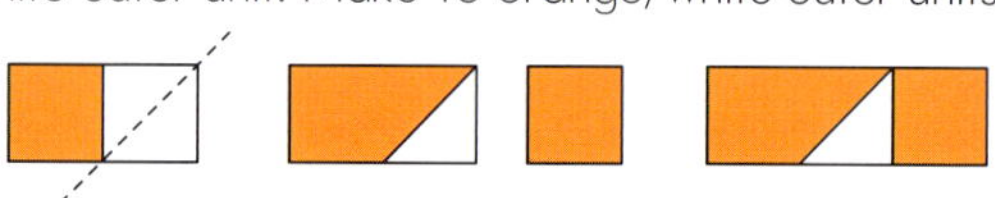

Make 16

4. Referring to step 3, make 4 white/orange outer units, 16 light aqua/dark teal outer units and 4 dark teal/light aqua outer units.

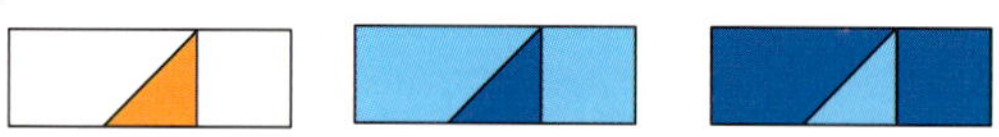

Make 4 Make 16 Make 4

5. Lay out 2 orange/white outer units and 1 orange/white/orange center unit as shown. Sew the units together to make an orange/white star unit and press. Make 8 orange/white star units.

Make 8

6. Referring to step 5, make 2 white/orange star units, 8 light aqua/dark teal star units and 2 dark teal/light aqua star units. Each star unit should measure 6-1/2" square.

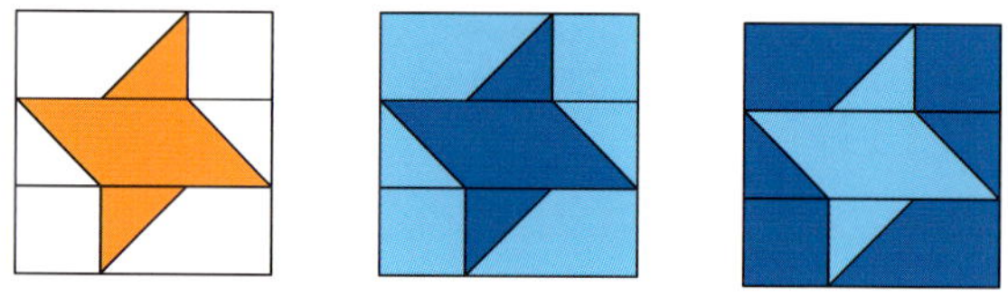

Make 2 Make 8 Make 2

Block Assembly

Note: Strips are added to the star units in alternating rows. The strips are trimmed after each addition.

1. With right sides together, sew a 2-1/2" x wof white strip to an orange/white star unit. Press the seam allowance toward the strip and trim away the excess fabric.

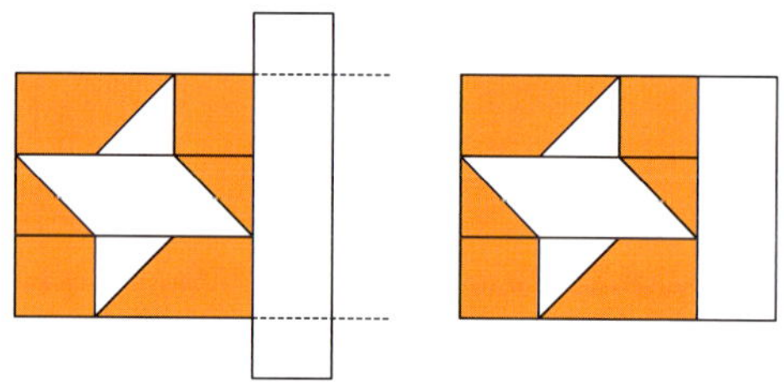

2. Turn the block a quarter turn to the right. With right sides together, sew the white strip to the orange/white star unit as shown. Press the seam allowance toward the strip and trim away the excess fabric.

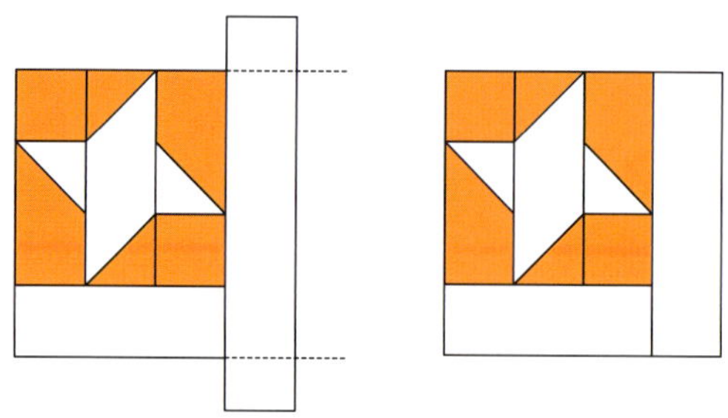

3. Referring to the illustrations, continue adding strips to the star unit in the same fashion, making sure the strips are only added to two sides of the star unit. Press and trim away the excess fabric from each strip as it is sewn to the unit. Sew a total of 6 strips to the star unit to make an orange/white block. Make 8 orange/white blocks.

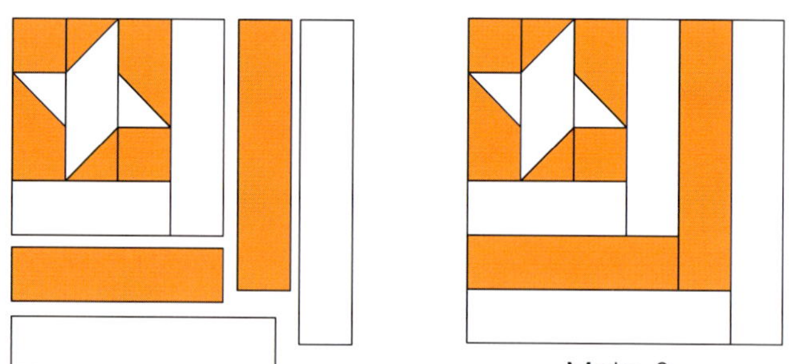

Make 8

4. Referring to step 3, make 2 white/orange blocks, 8 light aqua/dark teal blocks and 2 dark teal/light aqua blocks. Each block should measure 12-1/2" square.

Make 2

Make 8

Make 2

Quilt Center Assembly

1. Lay out the blocks in 5 rows with 4 blocks in each row. Refer to the Quilt Center Assembly Diagram for block orientation.
2. Sew the blocks together in rows. Press the seams in each row in alternating directions. Sew the rows together and press.

Finishing the Quilt

1. Cut the backing fabric in half crosswise to make 2 equal lengths. Using a 1/2" seam allowance, sew the pieces together along one long edge. Press seam open.
2. Layer the backing, batting and quilt top. Baste the layers together and hand or machine quilt.
3. Sew the binding strips together to make one continuous strip. Press the strip in half, wrong sides together, along the length. Sew the binding to the edges of the quilt. Turn the binding over the edge to the back of the quilt and hand or machine stitch in place.

Quilt Center Assembly Diagram

Wallhanging recreated by Laurel Albright; quilted by E.B. Updegraff

Inspired by Homespun Stars Quilt in Thimbleberries® Classic Country by Lynette Jensen.

The Color of Stars

Wallhanging

Finished size: 24" square

Materials

(9) 8-1/2" squares assorted solid fabrics for star blocks

(9) 5" squares assorted batik squares for star blocks

1 yard white print fabric for star block background, lattice strips, lattice posts and binding

1/8 yard paisley print fabric for star block centers

1 yard backing fabric

30" square batting

Fabric quantities based on 42"-44"-wide 100% cotton fabrics.

wof=width of fabric

Sew with a 1/4" seam allowance unless otherwise stated.

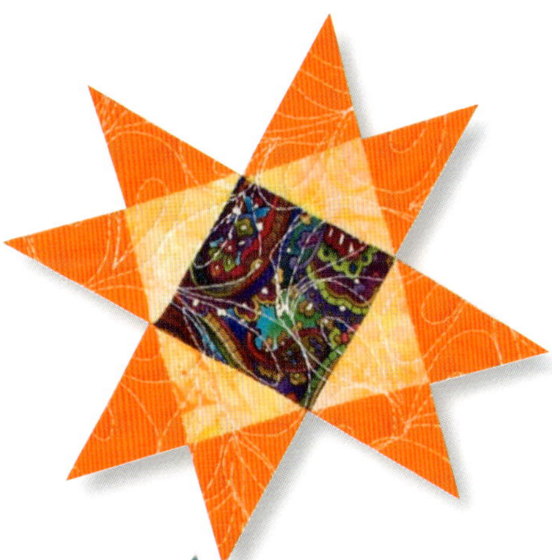

Cutting

From each assorted solid fabric square, cut:

(2) 3-1/4" squares. Cut the squares diagonally into quarters to make (8) D triangles. You need a total of (72) D triangles.

From each assorted batik square, cut:

(1) 3-1/4" square. Cut the square diagonally into quarters to make (4) C triangles. You need a total of (36) C triangles.

From white print fabric, cut:

(9) 3-1/4" squares. Cut the squares diagonally into quarters to make (36) A triangles.

(36) 2-1/2" B squares

(4) 2" x wof strips. From the strips cut:

(24) 2" x 6-1/2" lattice strips

(1) 2" x wof strip. From the strip cut:

(16) 2" squares for lattice posts

(3) 2-1/2" x wof strips for binding

From paisley print fabric, cut:

(9) 2-1/2" E squares

Star Block Assembly

1. Layer a solid D triangle and a white print A triangle right sides together. Stitch along the bias edge as shown. Be careful not to stretch the triangles. Press to make a DA triangle. Make 36 DA triangles.

Note: Always sew along the same bias edge and with the solid D triangle on top.

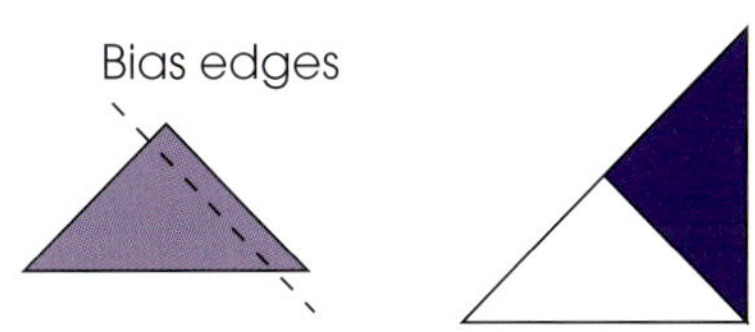

2. Layer a solid D triangle and a batik C triangle, right sides together. Stitch along the bias edge as shown. Be careful not to stretch the triangles. Press to make a DC triangle. Make 36 DC triangles.

Note: Always sew along the same bias edge and with the solid D triangle on top.

Make 36

3. Layer a DA and DC triangle right sides together, matching the center seam. Sew the triangles together along the long edge. Press to make a 2-1/2" star point unit. Make 36 star point units.

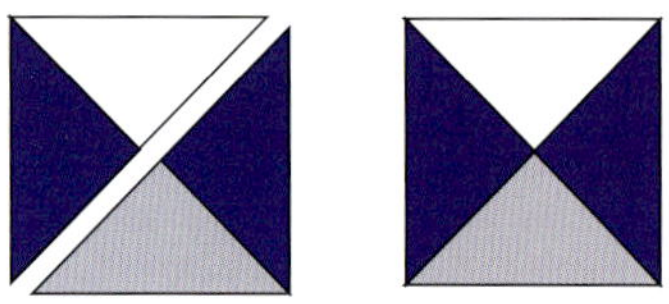

Make 36

4. Layer a white print 2-1/2" B square and a star point unit, right sides together. Sew the pieces together along the solid D triangle. Press. Repeat on the opposite side of the star point unit. Press to make a star row. Make 18 star rows.

Make 18

5. Layer a star point unit and paisley print 2-1/2" square, right sides together. Sew the pieces together along the batik C triangle. Press. Repeat on the opposite side of the paisley print square. Press to make a center star row. Make 9 center star rows.

Make 9

6. Lay out 2 star rows and 1 center star row as shown. Sew the rows together and press to make a 6-1/2" star block. Make 9 star blocks.

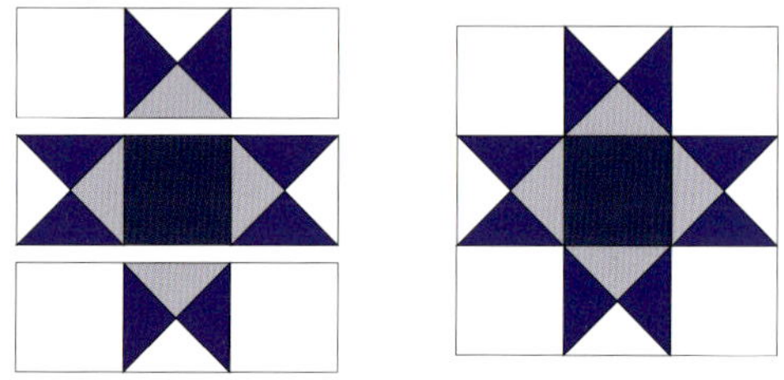

Make 9

Wallhanging Assembly

1. Lay out (4) 2" x 6-1/2" white print lattice strips and 3 star blocks in a row as shown. Sew the pieces together to make a block row. Press the seam allowances toward the lattice strips. Make 3 block rows.

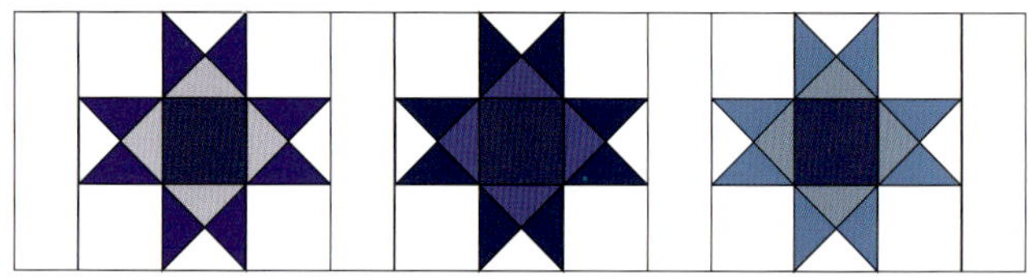

Make 3

2. Lay out (3) 2" x 6-1/2" white print lattice strips and (4) 2" white print lattice post squares in a row as shown. Sew the pieces together to make a sashing row. Press the seam allowances toward the lattice strips. Make 4 sashing rows.

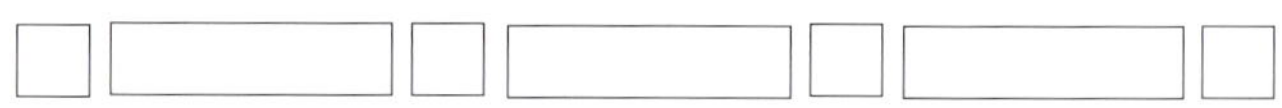

Make 4

3. Referring to the diagram, lay out the block and sashing rows as shown.

4. Sew the rows together, pinning at the seam intersections as needed. Press the seam allowances in one direction.

Finishing the Wallhanging

1. Layer the backing, batting and wallhanging top. Baste the layers together and hand or machine quilt.
2. Sew the binding strips together to make one continuous strip. Press the strip in half, wrong sides together, along the length. Sew the binding to the edges of the wallhanging. Turn the binding over the edge to the back of the wallhanging and hand or machine stitch in place.

Table square recreated and
quilted by Kitty Jacobson

Inspired by Star Table Square
in Thimbleberries® Four Seasons of
Calendar Table Toppers by Lynette Jensen.

Star

Table Square

Finished size: 45" square

Materials

3/8 yard white dot fabric for star block

7/8 yard red print fabric for star block and binding

1-3/8 yards gray print fabric for star block and outer border

1/2 yard dark gray print fabric for inner border and inner and middle border corner squares

3/8 yard white print fabric for inner border

1/2 yard black print fabric for middle border and outer border corner squares

3 yards backing fabric

49" square batting

Fabric quantities based on 42"-44"-wide 100% cotton fabrics.

wof=width of fabric

Sew with a 1/4" seam allowance unless otherwise stated.

Cutting

From white dot fabric, cut:

- (1) 6-7/8" x wof strip. From the strip cut:
  - (2) 6-7/8" squares. Cut the squares in half diagonally to make 4 large triangles.
- (4) 3-7/8" squares. Cut the squares in half diagonally to make 8 small triangles.
- (1) 3-7/8" x wof strip

From red print fabric, cut:

- (2) 3-7/8 x wof strips. From 1 strip cut:
  - (8) 3-7/8" squares. Cut the squares in half diagonally to make 16 small triangles.
- (5) 2-1/2" x wof strips for binding

From gray print fabric, cut:

- (1) 6-7/8" x wof strip. From the strip cut:
  - (4) 6-7/8" squares. Cut the squares in half diagonally to make 8 large triangles.
- (1) 6-1/2" x wof strip. From the strip cut:
  - (4) 6-1/2" squares
- (4) 6-1/2" x wof outer border strips

From dark gray print fabric, cut:

- (3) 3-1/2" x wof strips. From the strips cut:
  - (16) 3-1/2" x 6-1/2" rectangles
  - (4) 3-1/2" inner border corner squares
- (4) 2" middle border corner squares

From white print fabric, cut:

- (3) 3-1/2" x wof strips. From the strips cut:
  - (32) 3-1/2" squares

From black print fabric, cut:

- (1) 6-1/2" x wof strip. From the strip cut:
  - (4) 6-1/2" outer border corner squares
- (4) 2" x wof middle border strips

Star Block Assembly

1. Layer the white dot and red print 3-7/8" x wof strips right sides together. Press. Cut the layered strips into (6) 3-7/8" squares. Cut the squares in half diagonally to make 12 sets of triangles.

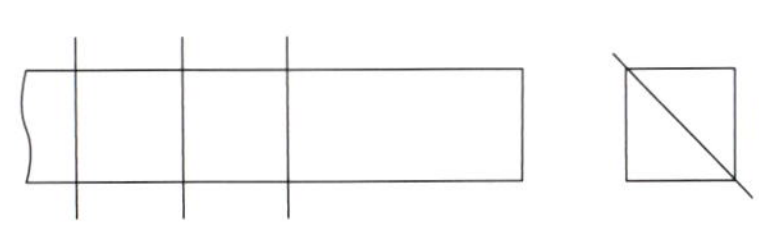

Make 12

2. Stitch 1/4" from the long edge of each set of triangles. Press the triangles open to make (12) 3-1/2" half-square triangles.

Make 12

3. Sew a small red print triangle to the half-square triangle's white dot edge as shown. Press. Sew another small red print triangle to the remaining white dot edge. Press. Make 4 units.

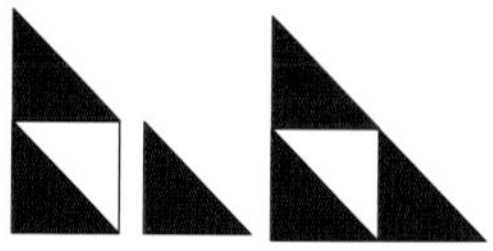

Make 4

4. Sew a large white dot triangle to the unit as shown. Press to make a 6-1/2" star center unit. Make 4 star center units.

Make 4

5. Referring to the diagram, sew the star center units together to make the star center. Press. The star center should measure 12-1/2" square.

6. Refer to step 3 to make 4 units. Sew a large gray print triangle to the unit as shown. Press to make a 6-1/2" star point unit. Make 4 star point units.

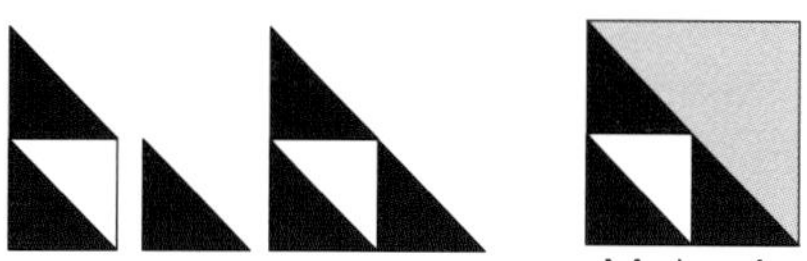

Make 4

7. Sew a small white dot triangle to the half-square triangle's red print edge as shown. Press. Sew another small white dot triangle to the remaining red print edge. Press. Make 4 units.

Make 4

8. Sew a large gray print triangle to the unit as shown. Press to make a 6-1/2" star point unit. Make 4 star point units.

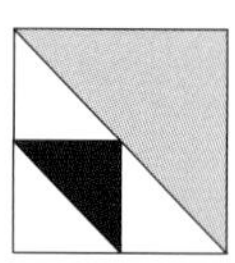

Make 4

9. Sew the star point units together in pairs. Press to make 4 star point sections.

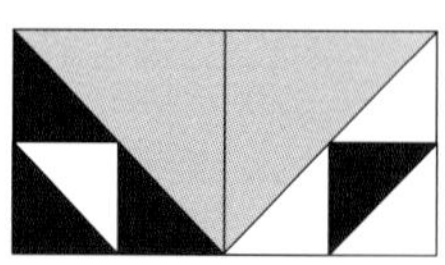

Make 4

10. Referring to the diagram, sew a star point section to the top and bottom edges of the star center. Press. Sew 6-1/2" gray print squares to the ends of the remaining star point sections and press. Sew these to the side edges of the star center and press. The star block should measure 24-1/2".

Border Assembly

1. Place a 3-1/2" white print square on one corner of a 3-1/2" x 6-1/2" dark gray print rectangle, right sides together. Draw a diagonal line, corner to corner, on the wrong side of the square. Stitch on the drawn line. Trim the seam allowance to 1/4" and press. Repeat with another 3-1/2" white print square on the opposite corner of the rectangle. Press to make a flying geese unit. Make 16 flying geese units.

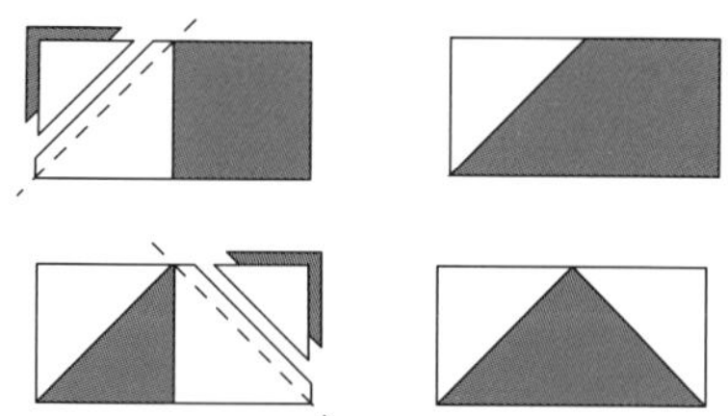

Make 16

2. Sew 4 flying geese units together as shown. Press to make a 3-1/2" x 24-1/2" inner border strip. Make 4 inner border strips.

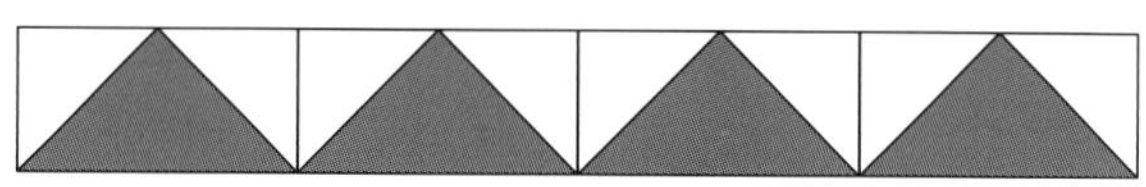

Make 4

3. Sew an inner border strip to the top and bottom edges of the star block. Press. Sew 3-1/2" dark gray print inner corner squares to both ends of the remaining inner border strips and press. Sew these to the side edges of the star block and press.

4. Sew 2" x wof black print middle border strips to the top and bottom edges of the quilt center. Press. Trim any excess fabric.

5. Measure the quilt top along each side. Include the seam allowances, but not the top and bottom borders. Cut the remaining 2" x wof black print middle border strips to this length. Sew a 2" dark gray print middle border corner square to both ends of the remaining middle border strips and press. Sew the border strips to the side edges of the quilt center and press.

6. Sew 6-1/2" x wof gray print outer border strips to the top and bottom edges of the quilt center. Press. Trim any excess fabric.

7. Measure the quilt top along each side. Include the seam allowances, but not the top and bottom borders. Cut the remaining 6-1/2" x wof gray print outer border strips to this length. Sew a 6-1/2" black print outer border corner square to both ends of the remaining middle border strips and press. Sew the border strips to the side edges of the quilt center and press.

Finishing the Quilt

1. Cut the backing fabric in half crosswise to make (2) 1-1/2 yard lengths. Using a 1/2" seam allowance, sew the pieces together along one long edge. Press seam open.

2. Layer the backing, batting and quilt top. Baste the layers together and hand or machine quilt.

3. Sew the binding strips together to make one continuous strip. Press the strip in half, wrong sides together, along the length. Sew the binding to the edges of the quilt. Turn the binding over the edge to the back of the quilt and hand or machine stitch in place.

Table runner recreated and quilted by E.B. Updegraff

Inspired by Star Studded Quilt in Thimbleberries® Small Wonders by Lynette Jensen.

Star Studded

Table Runner

Finished size: 19-1/2" x 56"

Materials

1/4 yard graphic print fabric for star blocks and block sides

1/4 yard medium gray print fabric for star blocks and block sides

1/4 yard teal print fabric for star blocks and block sides

3/4 yard newsprint fabric for star blocks, block sides and sashing

1/3 yard red print for star blocks and binding

1-2/3 yards backing fabric

23" x 59" batting

Fabric quantities based on 42"-44"-wide 100% cotton fabrics.

wof=width of fabric

Sew with a 1/4" seam allowance unless otherwise stated.

Cutting

From graphic print fabric, cut:

(3) 4-1/2" squares for star blocks
(24) 2-1/2" squares for star blocks
(2) 2-7/8" squares for star blocks
(2) 1-1/2" x wof strips for side border
(1) 1-1/2" x 16" strip for block side

From medium gray print, cut:

(9) 2-1/2" x 4-1/2" rectangles for star blocks
(6) 2-1/2" squares for star blocks
(2) 2-7/8" squares for star blocks
(2) 1" x wof strips for side border
(1) 1" x 16" strip for block side

From teal print, cut:

(9) 2-1/2" x 4-1/2" rectangles for star blocks
(16) 2-1/2" squares for star blocks
(2) 2-1/2" x wof strips for side border
(1) 2-1/2" x 16" strip for block side

From newsprint fabric, cut:

(12) 2-1/2" x 4-1/2" rectangles for star blocks
(24) 2-1/2" squares for star blocks
(6) 2-7/8" squares for star blocks
(3) 4-1/2" x 12-1/2" rectangles for block sides
(2) 2-1/2" x 16-1/2" strips for sashing
(2) 8-1/2" x 16-1/2" rectangles

From red print fabric, cut:

(6) 2-7/8" squares for star blocks
(12) 2-1/2" squares for star blocks
(6) 2-1/2" x 4-1/2" rectangles for star blocks
(5) 2-1/4" x wof strips for binding

Star Block Assembly

1. Place a 2-1/2" graphic print square on one corner of a 2-1/2" x 4-1/2" red print rectangle, right sides together. Draw a diagonal line, corner to corner, on the wrong side of the square. Stitch on the drawn line. Trim the seam allowance to 1/4" and press. Repeat with another 2-1/2" graphic print square on the opposite corner of the rectangle. Press to make a center star point unit. Make 3 graphic/red center star point units. Repeat to make 3 graphic/teal and 6 graphic/medium gray center star point units.

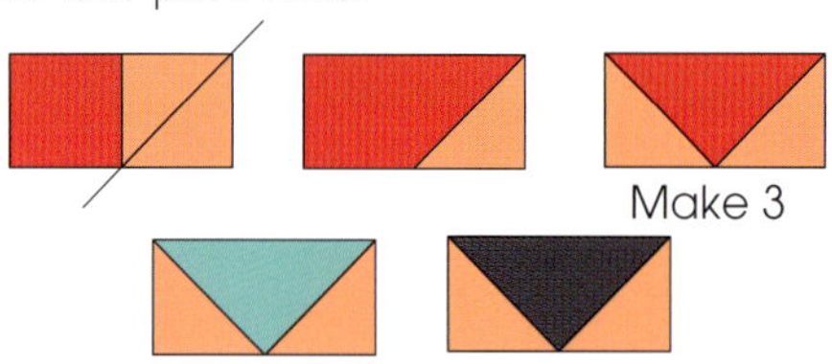

Make 3 Make 3 Make 6

2. Place a 2-1/2" red print square on one corner of a 2-1/2" x 4-1/2" newsprint rectangle, right sides together. Draw a diagonal line, corner to corner, on the wrong side of the square. Stitch on the drawn line. Trim the seam allowance to 1/4" and press. Repeat with another 2-1/2" red print square on the opposite corner of the rectangle. Press to make an outer star point unit. Make 6 red/newsprint outer star point units. Repeat to make 3 teal/newsprint and 3 medium gray/newsprint outer star point units.

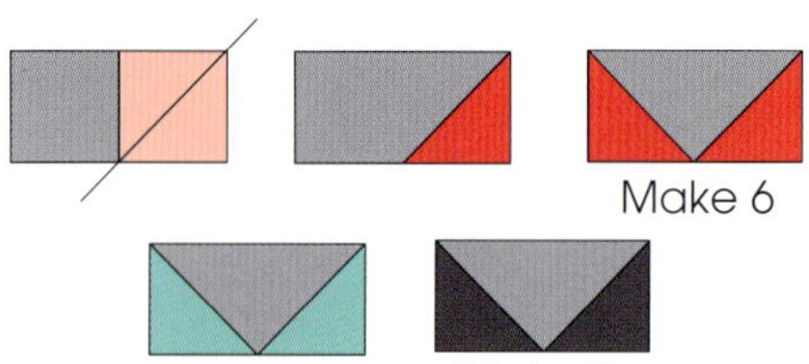

Make 6 Make 3 Make 3

3. Lay out a graphic/red center star point unit and a medium gray/newsprint outer star point unit as shown. Sew the units together to make star point A. Make 3 star point A.

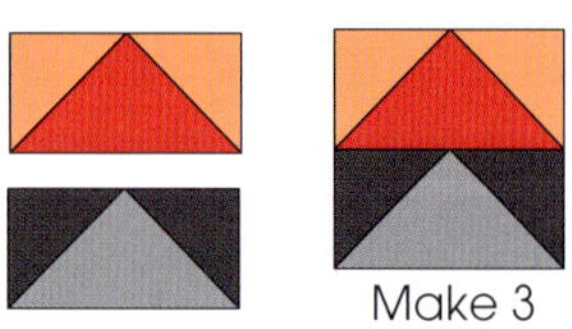

Make 3 star point A

4. Referring to step 3 and the diagrams, make 6 star point B and 3 star point C.

Make 6 star point B Make 3 star point C

5. Lay out a 4-1/2" graphic square, 1 star point C and 1 star point B as shown. Sew the pieces together to make a star center row. Make 3 star center rows. Each star center row should measure 4-1/2" x 12-1/2".

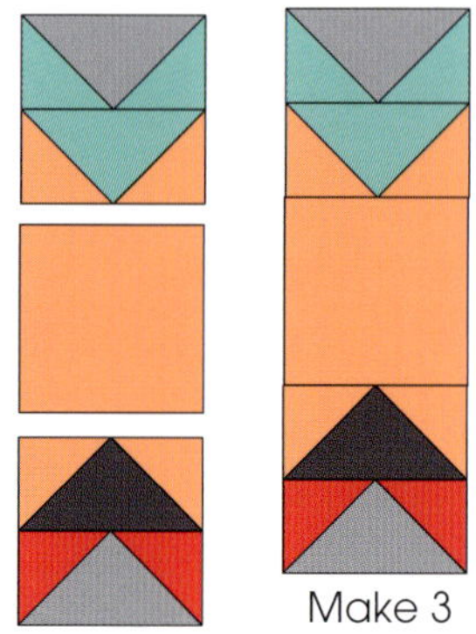

Make 3

6. With right sides together, lay a 2-1/2" newsprint square on the right corner of a 2-1/2" x 4-1/2" teal rectangle. Draw a diagonal line, corner to corner, on the wrong side of the square. Stitch on the drawn line. Trim the seam allowance to 1/4". Press to make a teal/newsprint unit. Make 6 teal/newsprint units.

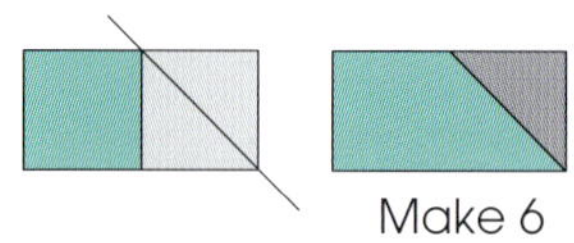

Make 6

7. Referring to step 6 and the diagrams, make 3 medium gray/newsprint units and 3 red/newsprint units.

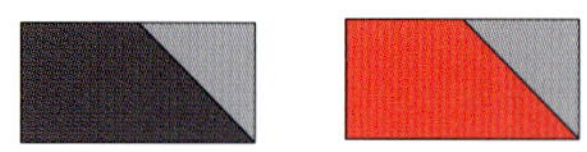

Make 3 Make 3

8. Layer a 2-7/8" red and 2-7/8" newsprint square, right sides together. Cut the layered squares in half diagonally to make 2 sets of triangles. Stitch 1/4" from the long edge of each triangle set. Press the pieces open to make (2) 2-1/2" red/newsprint half-square triangles. Make a total of (6) 2-1/2" red/newsprint half-square triangles.

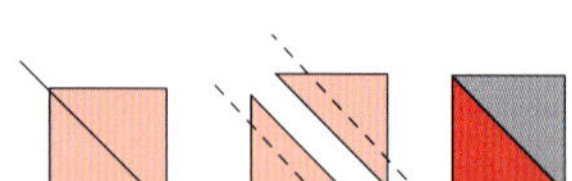

Make 6

9. Referring to step 8 and the diagrams, make (3) 2-1/2" graphic/newsprint and (3) 2-1/2" medium gray/newsprint half-square triangles.

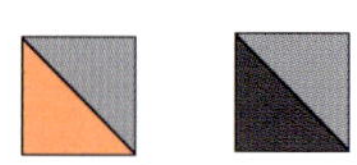

Make 3 Make 3

10. Sew a 2-1/2" newsprint square to the red edge of a red/newsprint half-square triangle as shown. Press. Make 6.

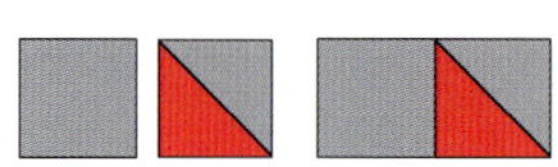

Make 6

11. With right sides together, sew the unit from step 10 and a medium gray/newsprint unit together. Press to make corner unit A. Make 3 corner unit A.

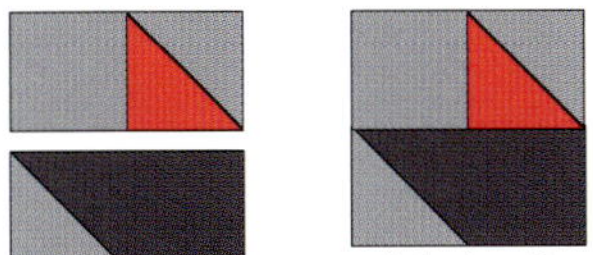

Make 3
corner unit A

12. Referring to steps 10 and 11 and the diagrams, make 3 corner unit B, 3 corner unit C and 3 corner unit D. Each corner unit should measure 4-1/2" square.

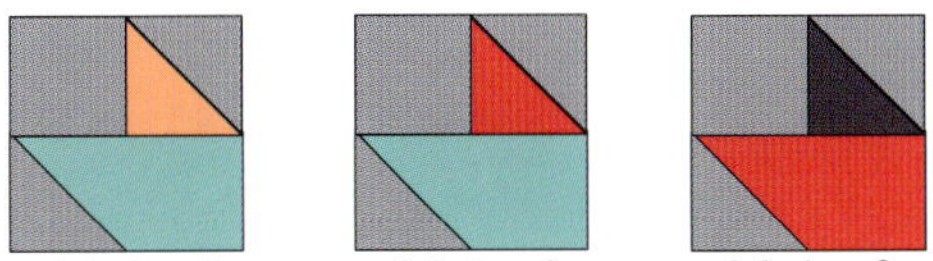

Make 3 corner unit B | Make 3 corner unit C | Make 3 corner unit D

13. Lay out corner unit A, star point A and corner unit B in a vertical row as shown. Sew the pieces together to make a left star row. Make 3 left star rows.

Make 3
left star rows

14. Referring to step 12 and the diagrams, lay out corner unit D, star point B and corner unit C as shown. Sew the pieces together to make a right star row. Make 3 right star rows.

Make 3
right star rows

15. Lay out a left star row, center star row and right star row as shown. Sew the rows together to make a star block. Press. Make 3 star blocks. Each block should measure 12-1/2" square.

Make 3

Table Runner Assembly

1. Sew a 4-1/2" x 12-1/2" newsprint rectangle to the left side of each star block. Press toward the rectangle.
2. Sew an 8-1/2" x 16-1/2" newsprint rectangle to the top of one star block and the bottom of another as shown in the Runner Diagram. Press toward the rectangle.
3. Sew a 2-1/2" x 16-1/2" newsprint sashing strip to the top and bottom of the remaining star block. Press toward the sashing strip.
4. Sew the three blocks together.

Side Border Assembly

1. Sew the 2-1/2" x wof teal strips together on the diagonal. Press the seam open.
2. Referring to step 1, sew the 1-1/2" x wof graphic print strips and the 1" x wof medium gray strips together in the same manner.
3. With right sides together, sew the teal and graphic print strip along one long edge. Press.
4. With right sides together, sew the medium gray strip to the remaining side of the graphic print strip. Press to make the side border.

Finishing the Table Runner

1. Sew the side border to the right side of the block unit. Press toward the side border. Trim any excess fabric.
2. Layer the backing, batting and table runner top. Baste the layers together and hand or machine quilt.
3. Sew the binding strips together to make one continuous strip. Press the strip in half, wrong sides together, along the length. Sew the binding to the edges of the table runner. Turn the binding over the edge to the back of the runner and hand or machine stitch in place.

Runner Diagram

Quilt recreated by Sue Voegtlin
and quilted by E.B. Updegraff

Inspired by Star Connection Quilt
in Thimbleberries® A Creative Christmas
by Lynette Jensen.

Jane's Star Garden

Quilt

Finished size: 59" x 73"

Materials

1 yard light blue print fabric for blocks

1-1/2 yards beige print fabric for blocks and borders

1-1/2 yards light cream floral print fabric for blocks and lattice segments

1-7/8 yards red/black stripe fabric for star points and outer border

4-1/2 yards backing fabric

63" x 77" batting

Fabric quantities based on 42"-44"-wide 100% cotton fabrics.

wof=width of fabric

Sew with a 1/4" seam allowance unless otherwise stated.

Cutting

From light blue print fabric, cut:
- (8) 2-1/2" x wof strips
- (3) 4-1/2" x wof strips. From the strips cut:
  - (20) 4-1/2" squares

From beige print fabric, cut:
- (14) 2-1/2" x wof strips. From 6 strips cut:
  - (14) 2-1/2" x 10-1/2" rectangles
- (18) 2-1/2" x 4-1/2" rectangles
- (4) 2-1/2" squares
- (6) 2-1/2" x wof inner border strips

From light cream floral print fabric, cut:
- (2) 6-1/2" x wof strips. From the strips cut:
  - (12) 6-1/2" squares
- (9) 4-1/2" x wof strips. From the strips cut:
  - (31) 4-1/2" x 10-1/2" rectangles

From red/black stripe fabric, cut:
- (11) 2-1/2" x wof strips. From 8 strips cut:
  - (124) 2-1/2" squares
  - From 3 strips cut:
  - (36) 2-1/2" squares
- (7) 3-1/2" x wof outer border strips
- (7) 2-1/2" x wof binding strips

Block Assembly

1. Layer a beige print and light blue print 2-1/2" x wof strip right sides together. Sew the strips together along one long edge. Press toward the light blue strip. In the same manner sew a beige print 2-1/2" x wof strip to the opposite side of the light blue strip. Press seam toward the light blue strip to make a strip set. Make 2 strip sets. Cut the strip sets into (24) 2-1/2" segments.

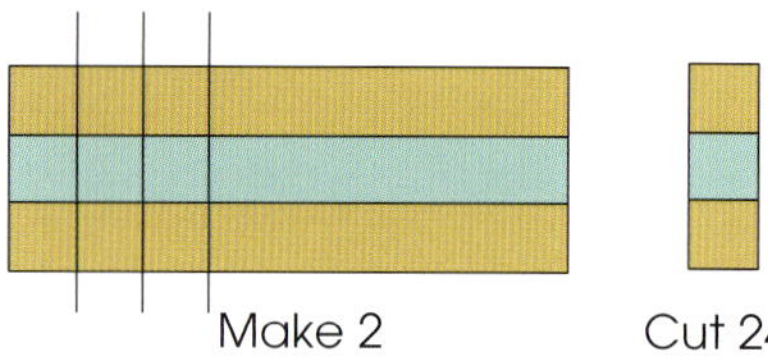

Make 2 Cut 24

2. Referring to step 1, sew (2) 2-1/2" x wof beige print strips and (3) 2-1/2" x wof light blue print strips together as shown to make a strip set. Make 2 strip sets pressing away from the beige print strips. Cut the strip sets into (24) 2-1/2" segments.

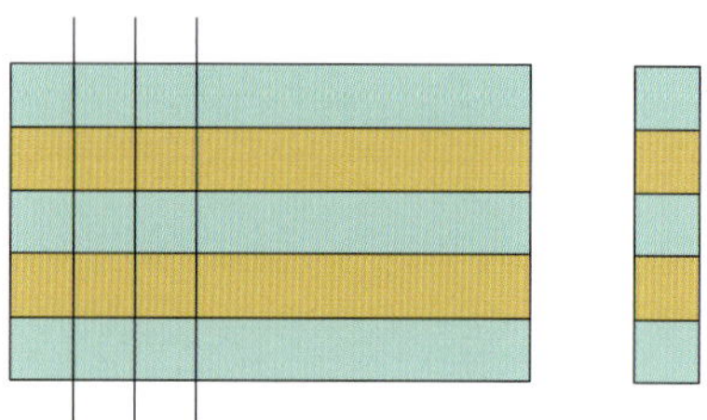

Make 2 Cut 24

3. Sew segments from step 1 to the top and bottom edges of a 6-1/2" light cream floral print square. Press toward square. Make 12.

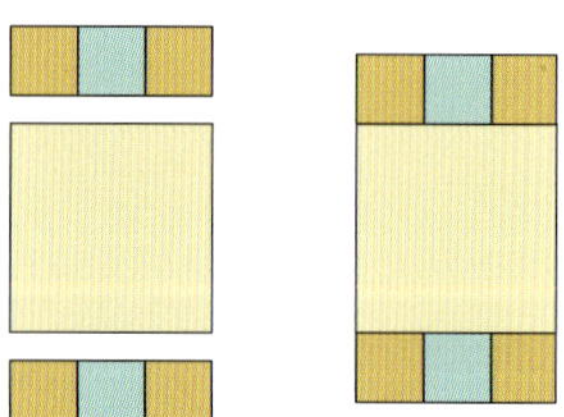

Make 12

4. Sew segments from step 2 to the remaining sides of the 6-1/2" light cream floral print square. Press. The block should measure 10-1/2" square. Make 12 blocks.

Make 12

Lattice Assembly

1. Place a 2-1/2" red/black stripe square on opposite corners of a 4-1/2" x 10-1/2" light cream floral print rectangle, right sides together. Draw a diagonal line, corner to corner on the wrong side of the squares. Stitch on the drawn line. Trim the seam allowances to 1/4" and press.

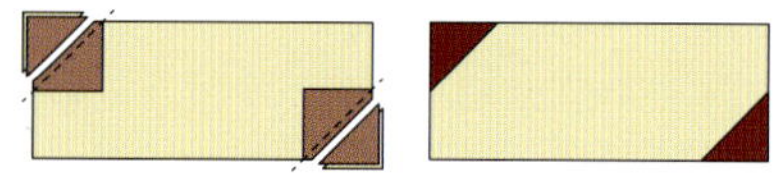

2. Referring to step 1, sew 2-1/2" red/black stripe squares on the remaining corners of the rectangle to complete a lattice segment. The lattice segment should measure 4-1/2" x 10-1/2". Make 31 lattice segments.

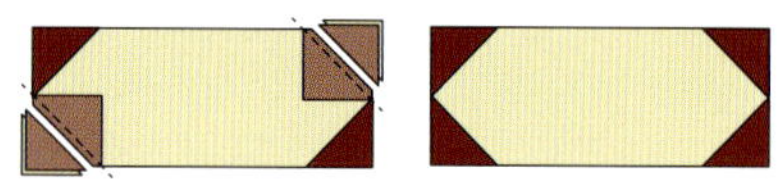

Make 31

Quilt Center Assembly

1. Lay out 4 lattice segments and 3 blocks as shown. Sew the pieces together to make a block row. Press the seams toward the blocks. The block row should measure 10-1/2" x 46-1/2". Make 4 block rows.

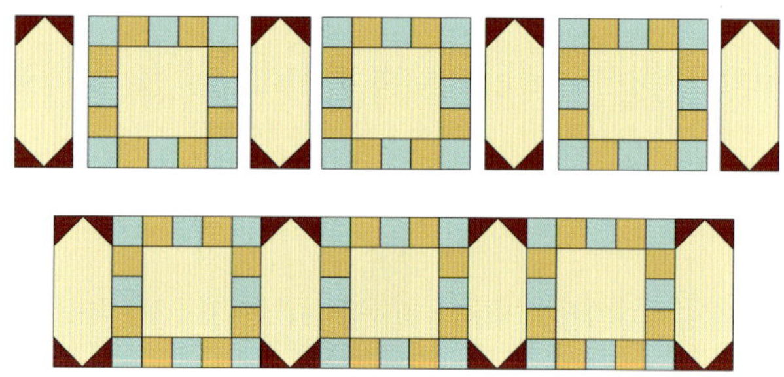

Make 4

2. Lay out (4) 4-1/2" light blue squares and 3 lattice segments as shown. Sew the pieces together to make a lattice strip. Press the seams toward the light blue squares. The lattice strip should measure 4-1/2" x 46-1/2". Make 5 lattice strips.

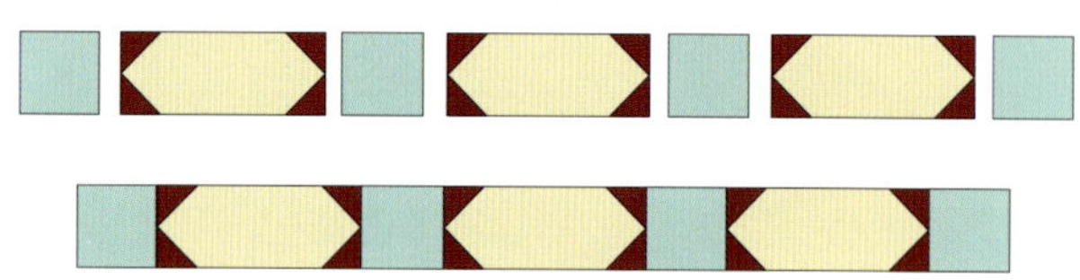

Make 5

3. Referring to the Quilt Center Assembly Diagram, lay out the block rows and lattice strips as shown.

4. Sew the rows together, pinning at the seam intersections as needed. Press the seam allowances in one direction. The quilt center should measure 46-1/2" x 60-1/2".

Quilt Center Assembly Diagram

Border Assembly

1. Place a 2-1/2" red/black stripe square on one corner of a 2-1/2" x 4-1/2" beige print rectangle. Draw a diagonal line, corner to corner, on the wrong side of the square. Stitch on the drawn line. Trim the seam allowance to 1/4" and press. Repeat with another 2-1/2" red/black stripe square on the opposite corner of the rectangle to make a star point unit. Make 18 star point units.

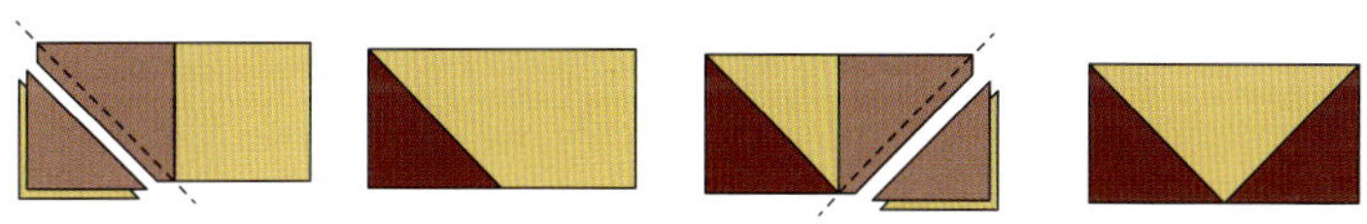

Make 18

2. Lay out 4 star point units and (3) 2-1/2" x 10-1/2" beige print rectangles. Sew the pieces together and press to make a top/bottom border strip as shown. The top/bottom border strip should measure 2-1/2" x 46-1/2". Make 2 top/bottom border strips.

Make 2

3. Lay out 5 star point units, (4) 2-1/2" x 10-1/2" beige print rectangles and (2) 2-1/2" beige print squares. Sew the pieces together and press to make a side border strip as shown. The side border strip should measure 2-1/2" x 64-1/2". Make 2 side border strips.

Make 2

4. Sew the top/bottom border strips to the top and bottom edges of the quilt center. Press.
5. Sew the side border strips to the side edges of the quilt center. Press.

6. Sew the (6) 2-1/2" x wof beige print inner border strips together to make one continuous strip. Measure the quilt center from side to side through the middle and cut a top and bottom border to this length. Sew the top and bottom borders to the quilt center. Press.
7. Measure the quilt center from top to bottom through the middle. Include the top and bottom borders in this measurement. Cut two side borders to this length. Sew the side borders to the quilt center. Press.
8. Refer to steps 6 and 7 to sew the red/black stripe outer border strips to the quilt center.

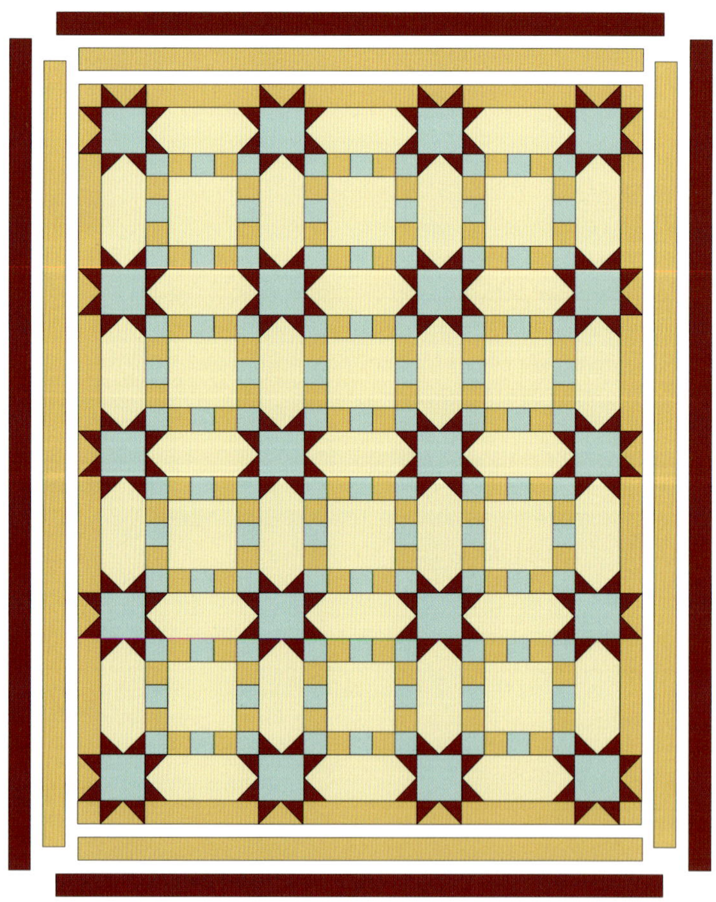

Finishing the Quilt

1. Cut the backing fabric in half crosswise to make 2 equal lengths. Using a 1/2" seam allowance, sew the pieces together along one long edge. Press seam open.
2. Layer the backing, batting and quilt top. Baste the layers together and hand or machine quilt.
3. Sew the binding strips together to make one continuous strip. Press the strip in half, wrong sides together, along the length. Sew the binding to the edges of the quilt. Turn the binding over the edge to the back of the quilt and hand or machine stitch in place.

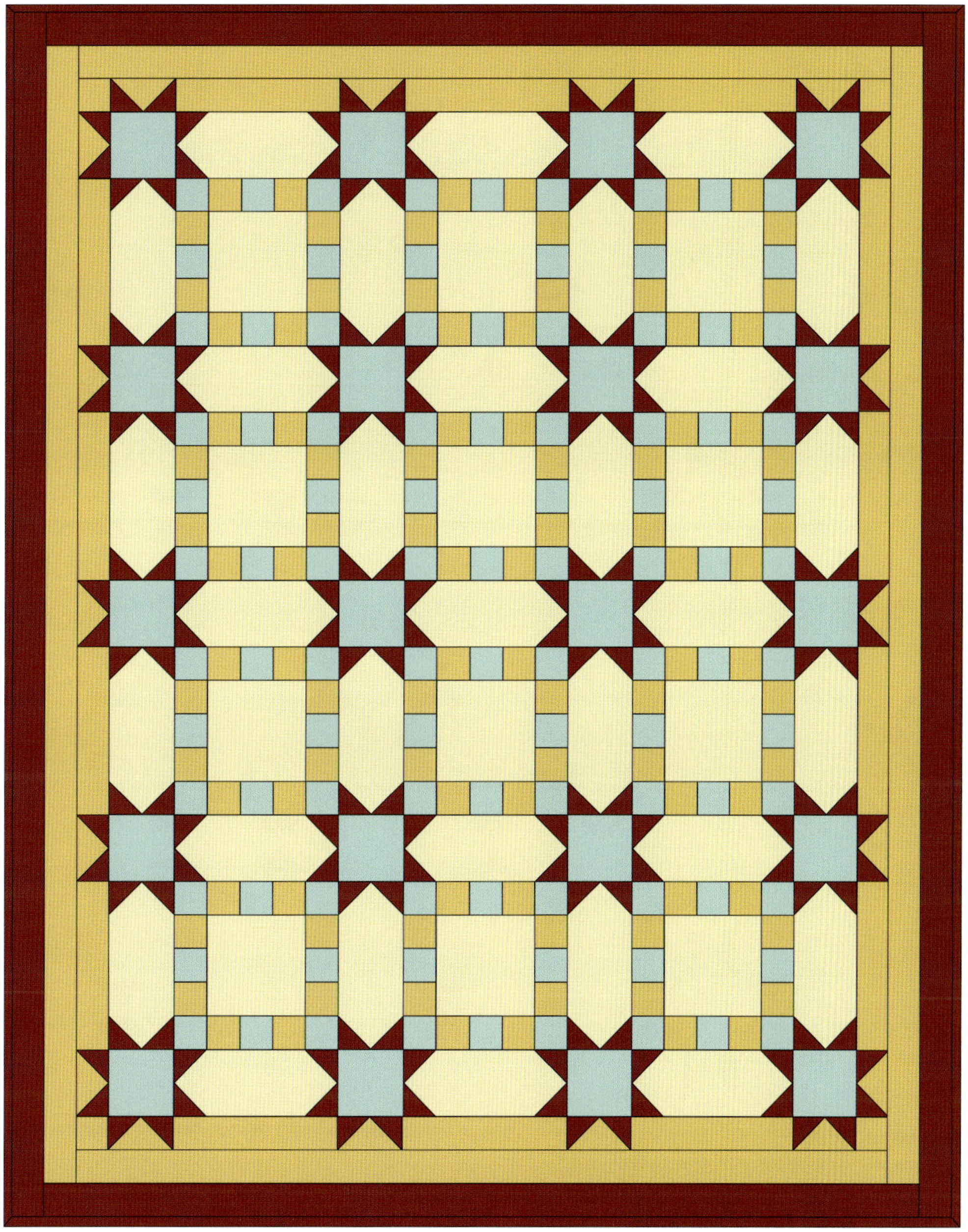

Quilt recreated and quilted by Sue Voegtlin

Inspired by September Stars Quilt in Thimbleberries® Collection of Classic Quilts by Lynette Jensen.

Star Steps

Quilt

Finished Size: 61" x 70"

Materials

4-1/4 yards beige batik fabric for star blocks, setting blocks, outer border blocks, borders and binding

5/8 yard red batik fabric for star blocks and outer border blocks

4-1/4 yards backing fabric

65" x 74" batting

Fabric quantities based on 42"-44"-wide 100% cotton fabrics.

wof=width of fabric

Sew with a 1/4" seam allowance unless otherwise stated.

Cutting

From beige batik fabric, cut:

- (6) 9-1/2" x wof strips. From the strips cut:
  - (24) 9-1/2" setting blocks
- (8) 3-1/2" x wof strips. From the strips cut:
  - (90) 3-1/2" squares
- (4) 4-1/4" x wof strips. From the strips cut:
  - (36) 4-1/4" squares. Cut the squares diagonally into quarters to make 144 quarter-square triangles.
- (6) 1-1/2" x wof inner border strips
- (6) 3" x wof strips. From 5 strips cut:
  - (2) 3" x 25" side outer border strips
  - (2) 3" x 13" side outer border strips
  - (2) 3" x 8" side outer border strips
  - (2) 3" x 24" top/bottom outer border strips
  - (2) 3" x 10" top/bottom outer border strips
  - (2) 3" x 6" top/bottom outer border strips
  - From 1 strip cut: (16) 3" squares
- (1) 3-3/4" x wof strip. From the strip cut:
  - (11) 3-3/4" squares. Cut the squares diagonally into quarters to make 44 quarter-square triangles.
- (7) 2-1/2" x wof binding strips
- From remaining beige batik fabric scraps, cut:
- (2) 3" squares
- (1) 3-3/4" square. Cut the square diagonally into quarters to make 4 quarter-square triangles.

From red batik fabric, cut:

- (4) 4-1/4" x wof strips. From the strips cut:
  - (36) 4-1/4" squares. Cut the squares diagonally into quarters to make 144 quarter-square triangles.
- (1) 3-3/4" x wof strip. From the strip cut:
  - (11) 3-3/4" squares. Cut the squares diagonally into quarters to make 44 quarter-square triangles.
- From remaining red batik fabric scraps, cut:
  - (1) 3-3/4" square. Cut the square diagonally into quarters to make 4 quarter-square triangles.

Star Block Assembly

1. Layer a 4-1/4" red batik triangle and a 4-1/4" beige batik triangle right sides together. Stitch along the bias edge as shown. Be careful not to stretch the triangles. Press to make a red/beige triangle. Make 144 red/beige triangles.

Note: Always sew along the same bias edge and with the red batik triangle on top.

Bias edges

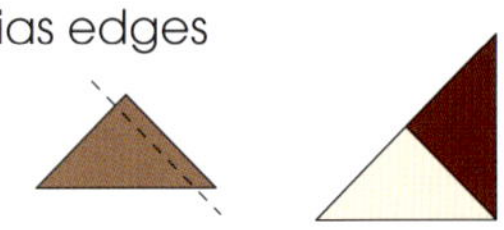

Make 144

2. Layer 2 red/beige triangles, right sides together, matching seams. Sew the triangles together along the long edge. Press to make a star point unit. The star point unit should measure 3-1/2". Make 72 star point units.

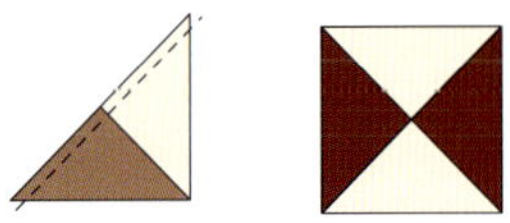

Make 72

3. Lay out (5) 3-1/2" beige batik squares and 4 star point units in three rows as shown.

4. Sew the pieces together in rows. Sew the rows together to make a star block. The star block should measure 9-1/2". Make 18 star blocks.

Make 18

Quilt Center Assembly

1 Referring to the Quilt Center Assembly Diagram, lay out the star blocks and 9-1/2" beige batik setting blocks in 7 rows with 6 blocks in each row.

2. Sew the blocks together in rows. Press the seams in each row in alternating directions. Sew the rows together and press to complete the quilt center.

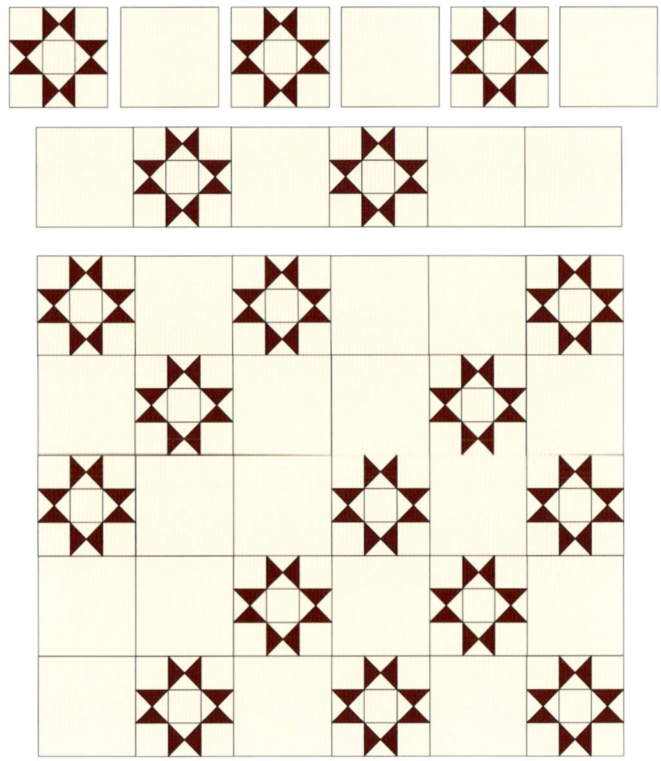

Quilt Center Assembly Diagram

Border Assembly

1. Sew the (6) 1-1/2" x wof beige batik inner border strips together to make one continuous strip. Measure the quilt center from side to side through the middle and cut a top and bottom border to this length. Sew the top and bottom borders to the quilt center. Press.

2. Measure the quilt center from top to bottom through the middle. Include the top and bottom borders in this measurement. Cut two side borders to this length. Sew the side borders to the quilt center. Press.

3. Layer a 3-3/4" red batik triangle and a 3-3/4" beige batik triangle right sides together. Stitch along the bias edge as shown. Be careful not to stretch the triangles. Press to make a red/beige triangle. Make 48 red/beige triangles.

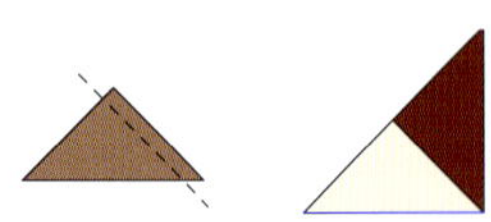

Make 48

Note: Always sew along the same bias edge and with the red batik triangle on top.

4. Layer 2 red/beige triangles, right sides together, matching seams. Sew the triangles together along the long edge. Press to make an outer border block. The outer border unit should measure 3". Make 24 outer border blocks.

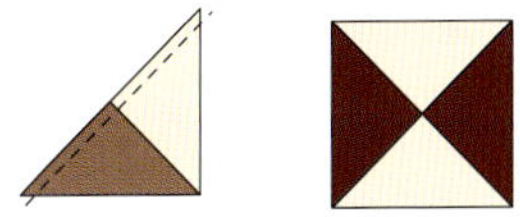

Make 24

5. Lay out 6 outer border blocks, (4) 3" beige batik squares, (1) 3" x 6" outer border strip, (1) 3" x 24" outer border strip and (1) 3" x 10" outer border strip in a row as shown. Sew the pieces together to make a top/bottom outer border strip. Make 2 top/bottom outer border strips.

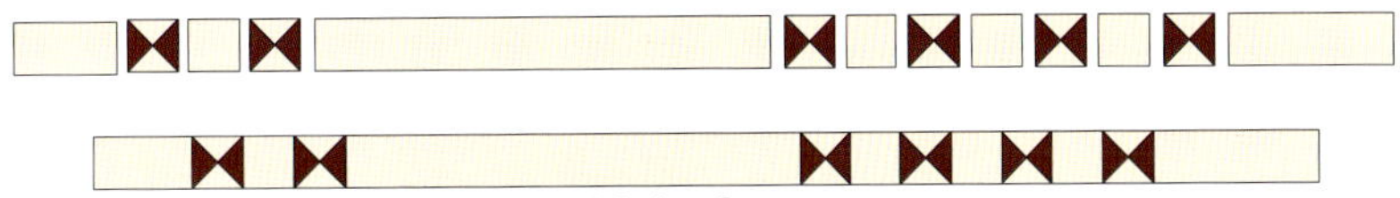

Make 2

6. Lay out 6 outer border blocks, (4) 3" beige batik squares, (1) 3" x 13" outer border strip, (1) 3" x 25" outer border strip and (1) 3" x 8" outer border strip in a row as shown. Sew the pieces together to make a side outer border strip. Make 2 side outer border strips.

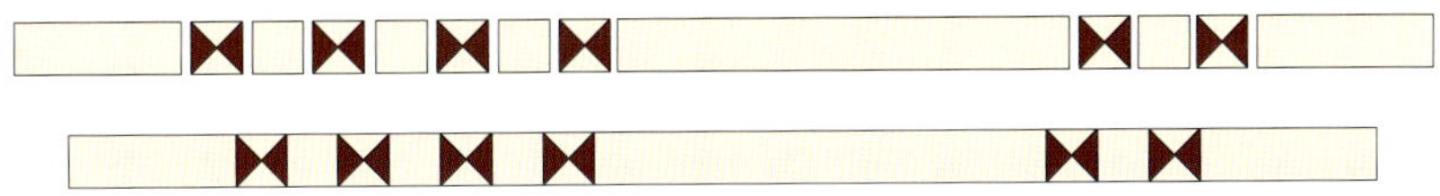

Make 2

7. Sew the side outer border strips to the sides of the quilt center. Press toward the borders. Trim any excess fabric.

8. Sew the top/bottom border strips to the top and bottom of the quilt center. Press toward the borders. Trim any excess fabric.

Finishing the Quilt

1. Cut the backing fabric in half crosswise to make 2 equal lengths. Using a 1/2" seam allowance, sew the pieces together along one long edge. Press seam open.

2. Layer the backing, batting and quilt top. Baste the layers together and hand or machine quilt.

3. Sew the binding strips together to make one continuous strip. Press the strip in half, wrong sides together, along the length. Sew the binding to the edges of the quilt. Turn the binding over the edge to the back of the quilt and hand or machine stitch in place.

Project	Inspiration

Project

Inspiration